Pittsburgh and the P & LE

ALFRED E. PERLMAN

"*Were American Newcomen to do naught else, our work is well done if we succeed in sharing with America a strengthened inspiration to continue the struggle towards a nobler Civilization— through wider knowledge and understanding of the hopes, ambitions, and deeds of leaders in the past who have upheld Civilization's material progress. As we look backward, let us look forward.*"

—CHARLES PENROSE
(1886-1958)
Senior Vice-President for North America
The Newcomen Society
for the study of the history of
Engineering and Technology
(1923-1957)
Chairman for North America
(1958)

❧

This statement, crystallizing a broad purpose of the society, was first read at the Newcomen Meeting at New York World's Fair on August 5, 1939, when American Newcomen were guests of The British Government

"*Actorum Memores simul affectamus Agenda*"

An Address at Pittsburgh

P&LE'S FIRST LOCOMOTIVE

AMERICAN NEWCOMEN *through the years has honored numerous distinguished rail transportation companies, both in the United States of America and in Canada; and has honored the memories of pioneers who created these enterprises, as well as those who followed. Such a Newcomen manuscript is this, dealing with the beginnings, growth and contributions of the "Little Giant," an important railroad corporation now in its 85th year of service in the Nation's principal center of heavy industry.*

ᕯ   ᕯ

Colonel James M. Schoonmaker—One of the early group that promoted the P&LE. He was a director of the company during a continuous period of 50 years, from its beginning in 1877 to 1927. Placed in charge of the company in 1896, for the next 25 years he was Mr. P&LE himself.

Pittsburgh and the P & LE

ALFRED E. PERLMAN

MEMBER OF THE NEWCOMEN SOCIETY

PRESIDENT

THE NEW YORK CENTRAL SYSTEM

CHAIRMAN OF THE BOARD

THE PITTSBURGH AND LAKE ERIE RAILROAD COMPANY

THE NEWCOMEN SOCIETY IN NORTH AMERICA

NEW YORK   DOWNINGTOWN   PRINCETON   PORTLAND

1963

This Newcomen Address, dealing with the his-
tory of The Pittsburgh and Lake Erie Railroad
Company, was delivered at the "1963 Pitts-
burgh Dinner" of The Newcomen Society in
North America, held in Duquesne Club, at
Pittsburgh, Pennsylvania, U.S.A., when Mr.
Perlman was the guest of honor,
on June 6, 1963.

૭

SET UP, PRINTED AND BOUND IN THE UNITED STATES
OF AMERICA FOR THE NEWCOMEN SOCIETY IN
NORTH AMERICA BY PRINCETON UNIVERSITY PRESS
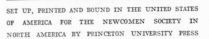

INTRODUCTION OF MR. PERLMAN AT PITTSBURGH, ON
JUNE 6, 1963 BY EDWIN HODGE, JR., CHAIRMAN, WEST-
INGHOUSE AIR BRAKE COMPANY; CHAIRMAN AND PRESI-
DENT, PITTSBURGH FORGINGS COMPANY AND GREENVILLE
STEEL CAR COMPANY; MEMBER OF THE PITTSBURGH COM-
MITTEE IN THE NEWCOMEN SOCIETY IN NORTH AMERICA

My fellow members of Newcomen:

WE welcome tonight Mr. Alfred E. Perlman, Chairman of the Board of the Pittsburgh and Lake Erie Railroad, and President of the New York Central Railroad Company.

Mr. Perlman is a member of the class of 1923 of Massachusetts Institute of Technology. The Institute fostered in Mr. Perlman that deep interest in engineering and technological research which he has effectively used in his career. In 1931 he took graduate work at Harvard's renowned School of Business Administration, where he studied under those profound students of transportation, William J. Cunningham and William Z. Ripley.

In fact, his railroad career began even before he entered M.I.T. He is a native of Minnesota who chose his career at the age of five, and it has since been his chief hobby. He started work at age 15 as an engine wiper in a round house of the Minneapolis & St.

Louis Railroad. It was only a summer job, but it was 12 hours a day. The next summer he was a coach cleaner for the Milwaukee Road, and the following summer he was in the employ of the Soo Line earning $30 a month.

Upon graduation from M.I.T., Al became a full-time employee of the Northern Pacific, and was soon working on the construction of a line extension into the Rosebud coal fields of eastern Montana. He then served on various parts of that system, in the mountainous areas of western Montana, northern Idaho, and the plains of North and South Dakota and Minnesota, but he never lost his basic interest as an engineer in track and structures.

His service on the Northern Pacific was interrupted in November 1934 when the Chairman of the Reconstruction Finance Corporation, Mr. Jesse H. Jones, sought Al's services for six months of special studies of some of the then ailing railroads, beginning with the New Haven Railroad. He there developed the first comprehensive scheme for the use of off-track equipment, with the consequent immediate savings of nearly one million dollars a year for that railroad, and at a time when a million dollars a year was real money.

The distinguished President of the Burlington, Mr. Ralph Budd, invited Al, at the conclusion of his R.F.C. assignment, to join his organization—which was jointly owned by the Northern Pacific and Great Northern Railways. The day before his arrival on the CB&Q—it was in May 1935—the entire main line from Denver, Colo. to western Nebraska was destroyed by a flood, and was completely out of service for a month. Al's job was to rebuild the railroad on an improved alignment and restore the service.

Not long after that the Denver and Rio Grande went into bankruptcy for the fourth time. It had never paid a dividend in the seventy-six years of its existence. Al was again borrowed—this time to prepare a comprehensive program for the rehabilitation of that railroad. He filled this assignment so adequately that he was invited to carry out his own recommendations. He took what he thought was a two-year leave of absence from the Burlington, but he became so intrigued with the problems of the Rio Grande that he remained there for 18 years.

The Rio Grande operates under the most difficult conditions of grades and curvatures, and at high altitudes. But despite its natural handicaps, Al formulated policies and programs that made the Rio Grande outstanding by every measurement of efficiency. He was instrumental in having the Rio Grande, and later the New York Central, establish a research laboratory, which he staffed with men and women of outstanding scientific qualifications. After twelve years, the railroad was completely revitalized and became one of the most prosperous in the Country. As evidence of this success, its stock was split three times within a period of six years.

In the spring of 1954, during the much-publicized fight for control of New York Central, Robert R. Young was asked, at a well-attended luncheon, "If you win the proxy fight, who will you invite to run the Central?" Mr. Young replied, "Al Perlman." The Dow Jones ticker carried the story immediately, and a call came in to Denver: "Mr. Perlman?" "Yes." "This is the editor of the *Wall Street Journal*. Is it true that Mr. Young has offered you the presidency of the New York Central?" "No." "How well do you know Mr. Young?" "I've never seen him; I've never talked to him; I've never met him." "Thank you."

Invited to New York to discuss the Central situation, Al was told that it was already 9 million in the red for the year and that it would have 6 million in the bank in January 1955 to meet a 35 million dollar payroll. Al was intrigued by the challenge.

The rest is well known: nearly half-a-billion spent in improvements; a new, young management team; and a reduction in debt of almost a quarter-billion dollars.

The impending consolidation of the New York Central and the Pennsylvania railroads promises to accomplish an objective Al has long cherished in the public interest. That is, the creation of three balanced competitive railroad systems in the east. I refer, of course, to the C&O-B&O system as one, the N&W-Nickel Plate-Wabash system as the second and the PRR-NYC as the third.

Gentlemen, MR. ALFRED PERLMAN.

James B. Yohe—General Manager 1906-1920; Vice-President and General Manager 1920-1929. A railroader's railroader who actually whipped the P&LE into shape and made it the "Little Giant."

My fellow members of Newcomen:

PITTSBURGH obtained its original impetus as a trading center, and its early military importance, from a strategic location at the point where the Allegheny River joins the Monongahela to form the Ohio. But it was the availability of extensive coal deposits that dictated Pittsburgh's pre-eminence as an iron and steel center and eventually brought the Pittsburgh and Lake Erie Railroad into being.

Iron making had commenced in the Pittsburgh region before the railroads came, but local deposits of iron ore were inadequate to support the rapid expansion of steel production that followed introduction of the Bessemer process in the 1860's. The availability in immense quantities of high-grade ore in the Lake Superior region enabled Pittsburgh, with its coal resources, to become the steel center of the Nation. The railroads were a necessary link in the chain of transportation that brought the iron ore to Pittsburgh. It may truthfully be said that the railroads built Pittsburgh, and with equal truth that Pittsburgh, in turn, built the railroads.

Born in the mid 1820's, railroads had established themselves by the 1850's. During the next decade they enabled the North to win the Civil War, partly by transporting ordnance products of the iron mills of Pittsburgh to points near the front lines. That the Northern iron horse ate coal instead of wood was a contributing factor to the victory.

The Civil War, like the wars of our own day, not only stimulated and accelerated invention and mechanization, but it also produced leaders, men of venturesome spirit who were willing to take risks. When the hostilities were over, many of these men devoted their energies and talents to railroad construction on a vast scale throughout the entire Country, especially in the rapidly opening West, where the challenges were the greatest.

The careers of these daring men are embedded in the post-war histories of our principal railroads. Soldiers such as General William Jackson Palmer, who used his great talents to build the Denver & Rio Grande, General Grenville M. Dodge, who pioneered in the building of the Union Pacific, and Colonel James M. Schoonmaker, of the P&LE, concerning whom I shall have more to say, are among those that should be mentioned.

The great industrial potential then opening for the Pittsburgh region offered all the necessary incentives for the expansion of railroad mileage in western Pennsylvania. The rough terrain of the western Allegheny slopes placed a premium on favorable railroad routes, and those along the great valleys of the Allegheny, the Monongahela, and the Ohio rivers were the most desirable.

By the mid 1870's each of these valleys had a railroad on one side or the other, leaving unoccupied, however, most of the south bank of the Ohio River between Pittsburgh and the mouth of the Beaver River. It was here that promoters of the P&LE planned to locate the principal segment of their proposed line between Pittsburgh and Youngstown. It is here also, though unanticipated at the time, that the great Aliquippa works of Jones and Laughlin Steel Corporation is now located.

The Pittsburgh and Lake Erie Railroad Company was chartered as a Pennsylvania corporation on May 18, 1875. Its route, like its present line, commenced on the South Side of Pittsburgh and followed the banks of the Monongahela and Ohio rivers northward to the mouth of the Beaver River, there to cross the

Ohio and follow the Beaver, and its tributary the Mahoning, to the Ohio state line, all on a water-level grade. An Ohio counterpart was organized to construct the eight-mile stretch within that state required to establish connections with railroads already at Youngstown. The Ohio company was soon merged with the Pennsylvania company to form the present company, which continues to be a corporation of both Pennsylvania and Ohio.

The prospects for a railroad in this location were good, but the promoters experienced the troubles promoters usually encounter, primarily lack of capital and effective leadership. The first President of the Pittsburgh and Lake Erie was William H. McCreery, then in the grain and commission business in Pittsburgh. He had already organized two small railroads that had been taken over by the Pennsylvania and had acquired financial interests in banks and iron furnaces. That he was chosen to head Pittsburgh's relief efforts following the great Johnstown flood in 1889 is some indication of his standing in the community as a civic leader. Among McCreery's associates in his efforts to get the P&LE started were John Bissell, who became secretary of the company, Captain John F. Dravo, a coal and riverboat man of wide interests, and Joshua Rhodes, a maker of steel pipe.

In the summer of 1877, while experiencing difficulties both in financing and in attempting to start construction within the two-year time limit set by the charter, McCreery, and eventually his official group, were succeeded by another more powerful group, including James I. Bennett, Henry W. Oliver, Jr., David Hostetter, and Col. James M. Schoonmaker.

Bennett, who took over the presidency from McCreery, was one of the wealthiest and most influential steel men in Pittsburgh. Oliver was already prominent in the steel business, and Hostetter had made a fortune in patent medicines, especially the famous "Hostetter's Bitters." Col. Schoonmaker, a Civil War veteran, was then prominent in the coke making business. The Colonel, who enlisted as a private and rose to be colonel of a cavalry regiment at age 20, was a colorful figure. He was tall, erect and courteous and had a variety of business interests. Some years later, in 1896, he was placed in charge of the company and for the next 25 years was Mr. P&LE himself. He was a director of the company during a continuous period of 50 years, 1877 to 1927.

Another person not to be overlooked in any account of the early days of the P&LE is Jacob Henrici, the venerable head of the Harmony Society, that strange combination of Christian communism, capitalism, and celibacy. At age 74, Henrici undertook to walk the entire 65-mile-length of the new line, and actually did walk one third of the distance in mid-winter, to inspect the construction work before trains were permitted to operate. As local residents are well aware, the Society's headquarters was at Economy, now Ambridge, Pennsylvania, a few miles down the Ohio River from Pittsburgh.

Despite the demand for a new rail outlet to the northwest, financial backing was hard to find during those years, especially since the Nation was in one of its severest depressions. The money required, between three and four million dollars to start with, was more than local people could raise, and outsiders, including English capitalists who were approached by McCreery, thought the project too risky without an affiliation with one of the larger companies already in existence.

Overtures were finally made to the Vanderbilts, who controlled, in addition to the New York Central and Hudson River Railroad, which carried their line to Buffalo, the Lake Shore and Michigan Southern, which provided the link to Chicago. The Lake Shore then had entrance into Youngstown, and could profit by a line into the Pittsburgh industrial area and an opportunity to reach the coal and coke regions to the south. The Lake Shore reached Youngstown through its tie with the Mahoning Coal Railroad, which extended from Youngstown to Ashtabula on Lake Erie, thus providing access to a harbor for lake traffic and a connection with the main New York-Chicago line.

In October 1877, two years after the company was organized, its future was assured when William H. Vanderbilt bought $300,-000 worth of P&LE stock. This substantial support from a prominent railroad capitalist encouraged others to subscribe. It was John Newell, the energetic manager of the Lake Shore, who is reputed to have gotten Mr. Vanderbilt, President of the Lake Shore as well as of the New York Central and Hudson River Railroad, interested in the P&LE. Newell station and Newell Yard on the P&LE are named after him.

Using the opportunities afforded him as one of the promoters and a large stockholder, Vanderbilt bought additional shares of P&LE as they became available. By the mid 1880's, he had acquired enough stock to control the P&LE and tie it to the New York Central System. That tie has continued to the present day.

Token construction of the main line, running 65 rail miles on easy grades along the Ohio, Beaver and Mahoning river valleys, was started inauspiciously in May 1877. There was no money to hire a contractor, so the road tried to pull itself up by its bootstraps by advertising that men could buy from one to four shares of stock and work out the cost "at fair prices for labor."

Construction started in earnest, however, in the fall of 1877 under a contract entered into on September 26 with B. J. McGrann, of Lancaster, Pennsylvania. He agreed to construct the road for $1,150,000 in cash, the same amount in bonds, and $200-000 in stock, a total of $2,500,000. The pace of McGrann's work displeased the directors, but eventually the main line was constructed and went into operation on February 12, 1879. The first train took 14 hours to get to Youngstown, but the first express, which followed about two weeks later, took only four hours to cover the same distance.

The company reported for 1879, the first year of operation, a profit of $157,500 out of revenues of $335,300, and for the second year a profit of $441,500 out of revenues of $840,500. For the third year, 1881, net earnings were reported as 14.2% upon the paid-in capital stock. Jacob Henrici, then President of the company, made no understatement in reporting to P&LE stockholders that this was "A result which in view of all the circumstances is very satisfactory." Modern accounting methods might have revealed a somewhat different picture, but clearly the enterprise was a success.

Perhaps the old gentleman in reporting "very satisfactory" earnings recalled that during the construction period he had driven a team of oxen from Economy to Pittsburgh, a distance of some 20 miles, in mid-winter to deliver a hoard of silver desperately needed to pay off workers. Acting paymaster Jones made this notation in his diary for December 21, 1878:

"I paid laborers constructing the New Castle branch, . . . A part of this money consisted of half dollars delivered in a wine keg and four bank bags. This money, bearing dates 1820 to 1860 was sunken in a well at West Economy, Pa., by the Economites when the Confederate General John Morgan made the daring raid across the State of Ohio."

The initial purpose of the P&LE was to provide a new rail line between Youngstown and Pittsburgh. The rail connections at Youngstown were satisfactory, but the line had no direct Pittsburgh outlet because a bridge had not been built across the Monongahela to provide a connection with the Baltimore & Ohio. The only connection was by ferry across the Monongahela River. It was soon evident that a direct access to the coal and coke regions of southwestern Pennsylvania was essential.

Pittsburgh's leading position as an iron and steel producing center was based upon the accessibility of coal that possessed superior qualities for making coke. The best coal of this type, and the largest quantities of it, were located in the Connellsville region, 50 miles south of Pittsburgh.

Connellsville region coal was converted into coke in long batteries of bee-hive ovens that surrounded the mines. Each oven held from five to seven tons of coal which was roasted in the closed brick retort to prevent combustion. The volatile matter was expelled, leaving the solid carbon as coke. The region was characterized by unpleasant clouds of smoke by day and picturesque pillars of fire by night.

The P&LE needed access to coke from the Connellsville area if it was to become and remain successful. An extension to the south was therefore undertaken through the chartering of the Pittsburgh, McKeesport and Youghiogheny Railroad Company on August 4, 1881. It was financed through advances made by the Vanderbilt interests. The PMcK&Y was completed by October, 1883, and had already been leased to the P&LE for a term of 999 years by a lease dated January 20, 1882. The stock of the PMcK-&Y is now owned equally by the P&LE and New York Central.

The PMcK&Y's line extends along the Monongahela River to McKeesport, Pa., a distance of 15 miles, thence up the Youghiogheny River to Connellsville, an additional 43 miles, where it now joins the Western Maryland. George Gould's transcontinental railway ambitions brought his Western Maryland into Connellsville in 1912 via an extension over the Alleghenies from Cumberland, Maryland. This connection with the Western Maryland affords the P&LE a southern outlet and the opportunity to participate in Baltimore and Philadelphia business.

The other segment of the PMcK&Y, now the more important one, extends from McKeesport along the Monongahela River, a distance of 38 miles, to Brownsville, Pa., where there is a connection with the Monongahela Railway. For all operating and traffic purposes, the PMcK&Y is regarded as an integral part of the P&LE.

The trend from bee-hive to by-product ovens for the production of coke, which set in after 1907, had traffic consequences for the P&LE. Bee-hive ovens must be located near the mines and away from cities and centers of industrial production. By-product ovens, on the other hand, should be adjacent to the principal points of consumption of the coke and of the by-product gas, which after extraction of coal tar chemicals, is used as fuel for blast and open hearth furnaces. With the decline in bee-hive coke production, Connellsville coke ceased to be such an important factor in P&LE traffic.

Like other railroads, the P&LE began with the kind of tracks, locomotives and cars that represented the minimum standards of the time. Just to start at all was the initial great achievement. However, a volume of traffic was immediately available that permitted rapid transformation into an efficient producer of transportation. Unlike many of its contemporaries, the original corporation has survived, without financial reorganization or change, down to the present time.

James B. Yohe was the man who actually whipped the P&LE into shape and made it the "Little Giant." Here was a railroader's railroader, a man who could organize work and manage men. Teamed with L. H. Turner, who was a superlative superintendent of motive power, men and machines were put together on the P&LE in a highly efficient working relationship.

Yohe's first railroad job—it was in the year 1870 and he was 14 years of age—was as a telegrapher on the Baltimore and Ohio's Pittsburgh and Connellsville Railroad at West Newton, Pa. Colonel Schoonmaker spotted him and brought him to the P&LE in 1883, soon after the PMcK&Y was opened. At age 27 he was already a seasoned railroader. For two decades, he was to all intents the general manager of the P&LE, but without the title. That came in 1906. In 1920, following federal control, and Col. Schoonmaker's retirement from active management, came the title of vice president and general manager. He earned no bachelor's degree in a college, but he held, in the esteem of his men, the honorary degrees of master and doctor of transportation. He was in his office early and late, and whether the dangers or obstacles were high water, landslides, or train wrecks, or even congestion on account of a flood of traffic, he was there on the ground directing the operations.

May I insert at this point that J. B. Yohe's son Curtis, C. M. Yohe, a friend of many here present, held the very same position as his father from May 1, 1929 to July 1, 1952, and remained a director until only last April.

A detailed account of the physical, traffic, service and financial developments of the P&LE from its earliest days to the present would be of book length. Measured over short periods, the changes were doubtless imperceptible, but in the perspective of time they are striking.

The history of any railroad, and the P&LE is a good example, could be told through the development of its locomotives. Progress in railroading is reflected in the increased ability of locomotives to haul more freight, and haul it faster. The very earliest locomotives, those of the late 1820's and 1830's—antedating the P&LE by half a century—had a capacity of about ten horsepower. By the late 1870's, when the P&LE's first locomotives were installed, their rating was in the order of 500 horsepower, and by 1897, when the P&LE pioneered in developing larger locomotives, the horsepower was about 1,500. Now 6,000 horsepower locomotives, composed, of course, of several diesel units, are commonplace, and there is nothing unusual in seeing aggregations of 10,000 to 20,000 horsepower hauling heavy trains up the long grades of western mountains.

As P&LE locomotives increased in size and capacity, tracks, bridges, and other structures were improved and strengthened. The standards of development of all other components of the railroad, both fixed and movable, auxiliary as well as basic, are tied to the locomotive. This is the unit, the prime mover, that establishes and maintains the mass transportation characteristics that constitute the true uniqueness of railroads.

Colonel Schoonmaker backed the building in the P&LE shops in 1897 of the celebrated No. 121 locomotive. It weighed 70 tons instead of 50 and pulled 2,500 tons instead of 1,500. In a test run against the conventional "Moguls" of the time its superiority was clearly proven. By 1903, the P&LE's average load per train was almost three times the average for the Country. Today, it is still a leader, with some of its trains hauling over 20,000 tons gross weight.

The P&LE also pioneered in car building. The first all steel hopper was built in P&LE shops in 1898. The company now has 9,000 all steel hopper cars.

The Ohio River bridge which was completed in 1910, was criticized for having more structural strength than appeared necessary at the time. But it is still a magnificent bridge, and the extra strength that was built into it and paid for 50 years ago now accommodates today's heaviest trains.

The P&LE has remained a small road. The 216 miles of line which it operates today are only one-tenth of one percent of the national railway system. Measured by dollar and other statistical yardsticks, the P&LE's operations do not produce impressive totals. The distinctions the P&LE has earned are of a different character.

The P&LE is a prime example of a railroad that has effectively utilized a favorable location to attract and hold traffic, and, through efficient operation, generate high earning power. Its income, and when necessary its credit, have been used to keep its plant and equipment up to date. The railroad has always been well maintained, and the latest technological and engineering improvements have been integrated into its fixed properties and rolling stock.

The best proof of this is the P&LE's car fleet. The P&LE serves, of course, the Nation's principal center of heavy industry, an area where both the volume and the proportion of originating tonnage are high. The rules and practices governing car service and supply make the originating line responsible for supplying cars required for loading. The P&LE, in order to meet the requirements of its patrons, therefore owns 25,000 freight cars. In relation to track mileage, tonnages handled, revenues earned, and other such factors, the P&LE's car fleet is larger than that of any other railroad. The railroads of the United States own 7.1 freight cars per mile of road; the P&LE owns 114. In fact, the aggregate length of the 25,000 cars owned by the P&LE equals or exceeds the length of its line.

But in this highly competitive era the mere number of a railroad's freight cars is not significant unless they are modern and in serviceable condition. Three-fourths of P&LE's fleet is less than 15 years old, and its bad order ratio is only slightly over one percent, an almost irreducible minimum. Eight thousand freight cars have been acquired by the P&LE in the past seven years at a cost of $72,000,000, and an order has been recently placed for 300 additional 70-ton capacity box cars. They will be 50 feet long, specially equipped, industrial type cars representing an investment of $4,350,000.

The P&LE has, in relation to its property and investment, earning power that places it alongside the Norfolk & Western, Union Pacific, and Santa Fe, which is to say, in the vanguard of the railroads of the United States. At the time this address was being prepared, its stock was selling within a point of its historic high. I shall, however, leave these details for a security analysts meeting rather than a Newcomen dinner.

Newcomen's interest in the history of corporate enterprises is intended to illuminate the pathway of the future. The progress of all industry is directly related to the rapidity, and the thoroughness, with which advances in technology and engineering are integrated into it. No industry possesses greater opportunities and potentialities than do the railroads for capitalizing on the developments that lie ahead. There are still many developments that railroads have not been able to fully utilize because national regulatory policy has denied them the traffic, and consequently the earning power, essential for them to do so.

Governmental policies have heretofore made political rather than economic considerations the basic determinants of railroad regulation. The railroads, all of them, from the most needy to the most successful companies, are equally dependent for survival as private institutions upon progress toward three basic objectives: first, consolidation; second, relaxation of rate regulation; and third, modernization of employee work rules. The outlook for the accomplishment of these objectives is more favorable than it has ever been. Whether favorable enough remains to be seen, but at least we view the future with hope.

The P&LE has been a Pittsburgh institution from its very inception. Some of Pittsburgh's most prominent citizens and benefactors, including James H. Reed, Philander C. Knox, Richard B. Mellon, and Richard K. Mellon, have served on its board of directors. Included on our present board are Thomas M. Evans, Chairman, H. K. Porter Company, Inc.; W. Cordes Snyder, Jr., Chairman and President, Blaw-Knox Company; William P. Snyder, III, President, Shenango, Inc.; Col. Willard F. Rockwell, Chairman, Rockwell Manufacturing Company, and Edwin Hodge, Jr., Chairman and President, Pittsburgh Forgings Company. "Ed" is our senior director, with 32 years of continuous service. Allison R. Maxwell, Jr., President, Pittsburgh Steel Company, has just accepted service as a Director at the meeting of the board here today.

An ex-Pittsburgher who still has Pittsburgh in his blood, John F. Nash, former President of the P&LE, who becomes Senior Vice-President of the New York Central on June 15, is a most active member of the Board.

John W. Barriger, President of the P&LE, who succeeded John Nash, is also a member of the P&LE board. John was born in Texas, was brought up in St. Louis, and lays claims, since his

Monon days, to being a Hoosier. However, he is now a staunch supporter of the Pennsylvania Society and has, in a short span of years, become a Pittsburgh institution.

The people of Pittsburgh are justly proud of the city's remarkable renaissance, the physical evidences of which are so strikingly exemplified by its "Golden Triangle." But buildings and bridges do not tell the whole story; the real renaissance is in the spirit of the men who planned and built the Pittsburgh of today and who are planning and building for the even greater Pittsburgh of tomorrow. We of the P&LE are proud to lay claim to a part of that Pittsburgh heritage.

THE END

❧

"Actorum Memores simul
affectamus Agenda!"

AN UNUSUAL P&LE INSPECTION CAR

THIS NEWCOMEN ADDRESS, *dealing with the history of* THE PITTSBURGH AND LAKE ERIE RAILROAD COMPANY, *was delivered at the "1963 Pittsburgh Dinner" of The Newcomen Society in North America, held at Pittsburgh, Pennsylvania, U.S.A., on June 6, 1963.* MR. PERLMAN, *the guest of honor, was introduced by* EDWIN HODGE, JR., *Chairman, Westinghouse Air Brake Company; President, Pittsburgh Steel Forgings Company and Greenville Steel Car Company; member of the Pittsburgh Committee in American Newcomen. The dinner was presided over by* W. CORDES SNYDER, JR., *Chairman of the Board and President, Blaw-Knox Company; Chairman of the Pittsburgh Committee in this international Society.*

≈   ≈

"The history of any railroad, and the P&LE is a good example, could be told through the development of its locomotives. Progress in railroading is reflected in the increased ability of locomotives to haul more freight, and haul it faster. The very earliest locomotives, those of the late 1820's and 1830's—antedating the P&LE by half a century—had a capacity of about ten horsepower. By the late 1870's, when the P&LE's first locomotives were installed, their rating was in the order of 500 horsepower, and by 1897, when the P&LE pioneered in developing larger locomotives, the horsepower was about 1,500. Now 6,000 horsepower locomotives, composed, of course, of several diesel units, are commonplace, and there is nothing unusual in seeing aggregations of 10,000 to 20,000 horsepower hauling heavy trains up the long grades of western mountains."

—ALFRED E. PERLMAN

❧   ❧

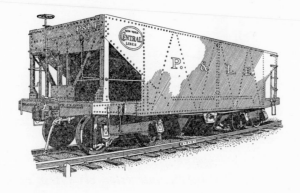

"The P&LE also pioneered in car building. The first all steel hopper was built in P&LE shops in 1898. The company now has 9,000 all steel hopper cars.

"The P&LE serves, of course, the Nation's principal center of heavy industry, an area where both the volume and the proportion of originating tonnage are high. The rules and practices governing car service and supply make the originating line responsible for supplying cars required for loading. The P&LE, in order to meet the requirements of its patrons, therefore owns 25,000 freight cars. In relation to track mileage, tonnages handled, revenues earned, and other such factors, the P&LE's car fleet is larger than that of any other railroad. The railroads of the United States own 7.1 freight cars per mile of road; the P&LE owns 114. In fact, the aggregate length of the 25,000 cars owned by the P&LE equals or exceeds the length of its line."

—Alfred E. Perlman

AMERICAN NEWCOMEN, *interested always in economic and transportation history, is happy in the opportunity to do honor to The Pittsburgh and Lake Erie Railroad Company and to its constructive history throughout 85 years. Rail transportation has made possible the amazing development of America's resources. Rail transportation has brought commerce and trade to every region of America. Rail transportation has contributed mightily to America's strength, wealth and greatness!*

THE NEWCOMEN SOCIETY
in North America

IN APRIL, 1923, *the late L. F. Loree (1858-1940) of New York, then dean of American railroad presidents, established a group now known as "American Newcomen" and interested in Material History, as distinguished from political history. Its objectives center in the beginnings, growth, development, contributions, and influence of Industry, Transportation, Communication, the Utilities, Mining, Agriculture, Banking, Finance, Economics, Insurance, Education, Invention, and the Law—these and correlated historical fields. In short, the background of those factors which have contributed or are contributing to the progress of Mankind.*

The Newcomen Society in North America is a non-profit membership corporation chartered in 1961 under the Charitable Law of the State of Maine, with headquarters on North Ship Road, Uwchlan Township, Chester County, Pennsylvania, some five miles east of Downingtown, Pennsylvania, and 32 miles west of the City of Philadelphia. Here also is located The Thomas Newcomen Memorial Library in Business History, a reference collection, including microfilm, open to the public for research and dealing with the subjects to which the Society devotes attention.

Meetings are held throughout the United States of America and across Canada at which Newcomen Addresses are presented by leaders in their respective fields. These manuscripts represent a broadest coverage of phases of Material History involved, both American and Canadian.

The approach in most cases has been a life-story of corporate organizations, interpreted through the ambitions, the successes and failures, and the ultimate achievements of those pioneers whose efforts laid the foundations of the particular enterprise.

The Society's name perpetuates the life and work of Thomas Newcomen (1663-1729), the British pioneer, whose valuable contributions in improvements to the newly invented Steam Engine brought him lasting fame in the field of the Mechanic Arts. The Newcomen Engines, whose period of use was from 1712 to 1775, paved a way for the Industrial Revolution. Newcomen's inventive genius preceded by more than 50 years the brilliant work in Steam by the world-famous James Watt.

The Newcomen Society in North America is affiliated with The Newcomen Society for the Study of the History of Engineering and Technology, with offices at The Science Museum, South Kensington, London, S.W. 7, England. The Society is also associated in union with the Royal Society for the Encouragement of Arts, Manufactures and Commerce, whose offices are at 6 John Adam Street, London, W.C. 2, England.

🎺 🎺

Members of American Newcomen, when in Europe, are invited by the Dartmouth Newcomen Association to visit the home of Thomas Newcomen at Dartmouth in South Devonshire, England, where the festival of "Newcomen Day" is celebrated each year on the fourth Friday in July.

※

"The roads you travel so briskly
lead out of dim antiquity,
and you study the past chiefly because
of its bearing on the living present
and its promise for the future."

—LIEUTENANT GENERAL JAMES G. HARBORD,
K.C.M.G., D.S.M., LL.D., U.S. ARMY (RET.)

(1866-1947)

Late American Member of Council at London
The Newcomen Society
for the study of the history of
Engineering and Technology

※